AF572131

Being a Father

Being a Father

poems by

Michael S. Glaser

Forest Woods Media Productions, Inc.
The Bunny and the Crocodile Press
for Seasonings Press

for information: Seasonings Press c/o
Box 1
St. Mary's City, MD 20686

Library of Congress Cataloging-in-Publication Data
Glaser, Michael S., 1943 -
Being a Father / Michael S. Glaser 1st edition.

p. cm.
International Standard Book Number: 0-938572-42-3
1. Glaser, Michael 2. Poetry 3. Parenting
I. Title
Library of Congress Control Number 2004102109

Published August 1, 2004
Second Printing, July 2005

Cover Design by *In Support Graphics*, Cindy and Ed Comitz
Typography and book design by Katie Coursey

Printing by George Klear, Printing Press Inc.

Acknowledgments:

Cover Photo of Adalyn Joy Glaser by Joshua Glaser.

Appreciations for advice and encouragement are warmly acknowledged to the many people who have supported the creation of this manuscript: my family, especially Kathleen; Grace Cavalieri, Lucille Clifton, John and Sandy Feneley, CMRS, Ken Flynn, Judith Hall, Wayne Karlin, E. Ethelbert Miller, Kaia Sand, Edgar Silex, Max Smith and St. Mary's College of Maryland for years of nurture and support.

Grateful acknowledgment is made to the editors of the following in which some of these poems first appeared, often in earlier versions.

America: Pony Tail
The American Scholar: Angels of Sunlight, Curator of Dreams
A Lover's Eye, *The Bunny and the Crocodile Press, Inc.*: Squinting Against the Light, On Being a Father
Anthropology and Humanism: My Daughter Dancing
The Christian Science Monitor: Fathers, Delta 1530, Thoughts on My Late-Born Child, A Note to My Wife, Beginning this Day, Migration, At Duntulm Castle, Toenails
The Christian Century: Images, Loss
Circus Maximus: Childmasks
Fathers & Daughters/Mothers & Sons (Papier Maché Press) Gathering Chestnuts
Hyacinths and Biscuits: I Watch You Emerge
New Letters: Report Card
Outsiders (Milkweed editions): Magnificat!
Palo Alto Review: Apple of Your Mother's Eye
Piedmont Literary Review: Shoes
Poem: Amira
Prairie Schooner: Children of Eden
The Silenus (The Feneley Library Press, Oxford, England), Magnificat!
Ruby: Before the 3:00 A.M. Feeding

Table of Contents:

Being a Father

I. Squinting Against the Light

II: The Curator of Dreams

III: In its Thinness, the Air is full

****

For

Brian

Joshua

Daniel

Amira

Eva

Sine qua non -- each one

I

Squinting Against the Light

Squinting Against the Light

The sky sows snow and sleet, though crocuses
poke purple heads through crusty soil.
Above, geese call their way north
        spreading awkward V's into the open sky.

A slowing, a pause, as if you wait — perhaps
for the sleet to pass, perhaps for tomorrow.
Your clock is not ours, your rhythms your own
        until your head breaks the salty waters

and your mother stops, tends to the pressure
of you as she will a hundred hundred times again,
remembering this rush between her legs,
        the rush of you, headlong toward the world.

And when your head begins to crown,
one ear, misshapened, protrudes into
my fears, then unfolds
        a petal into its own perfection —

Your head enters the doctor's hands, is turned
then a last contraction squeezes your shoulders
out and you glide into the world
        a sea creature, all the pieces in place.

I cradle you in my hands. Your face squints
against the light. Your eyes open, then close again
as your arms and legs flail their first
        flailing into the world, against the world.

Before the 3:00 A.M. Feeding

I lift you
into the ocean
of my love.

Your skin floats
on the waves
of each breath
you take

and your legs
drift down my arms
like the tide.

You meet the world
with your mouth
as you wake

and your lips,
clinging to the side
of my thumb,

make me wish once again
for an ocean of things
I can never become.

I Watch You Emerge

I watch you emerge,
running, grinning, skipping
your energy down the hallway.

You are a motorcycle,
a garbage truck, a curly-
haired dragon, vrooommming

your engines 'round the corner
and spilling your laughter
into the sunlight of my eyes.

Nightmare

In nightmare terror
you cry out: "DADDY!"

and I rush like Lancelot
from other dreams
to save you from your plight.

Arm in soothing arm we lie
against the slanted hues of night,
your breathing takes on gentle sounds
as darkness gropes toward light.

I hear you
yawn nearer
surrender to sleep

then you nudge away my armor
with your elbow, fist or feet.

I think of swift white chargers,
bloody dragons in defeat,
you turn your back quite suddenly,
fall separately asleep.

Gathering Chestnuts

When chestnuts fall, their pods open
to heart and egg-shaped gems — nuts smooth
and shiny, with leathery skin.

Come Christmas, we will roast them, but for now
they are gathered as best we can. We sit
at the kitchen table. While I slice vegetables

for dinner, my daughter examines each chestnut,
putting these into egg cartons, placing those
back in their pods like puzzle pieces

before taking them out again, rearranging them,
feeling their smooth skin, turning them over
and over until she seems to know for certain

just where each should go. I marvel at her
strategies — how her tiny fingers release
each from its shell, determine for each

its place with such confident grace, such
grown-up busy-ness, absorbed in detail
and task. We talk and work until our thoughts

take us away in the silence of hands moving.
And when I look again her way, I see her
facing me like a mirror, her elbow propped

on the table, like mine, her arm curved
into a question mark, her small hand,
a loose-fisted rest for her head. She grins

and I smile back, seeing myself reflected
in her brown, chestnut eyes, imagining she sees
herself, for this unguarded instant, in mine.

Childmasks

Words emerge from your mouth like locusts
Impatient to escape the plagues
Your body sprints from room to room
On wound and wiry legs.

The day affords no calm nor peace
And night brings jungle beings,
They toss and twist your curly head
And stalk the caverns of your dreams.

Sometimes, when they surprise you,
And startle you from sleep
Your body tumbles toward my bed
Impelled by errant feet.

When I wake to the touch
Of your hand on my skin,
My big arms yawn like jaws
And slowly let you in.

You name me
Big-bear-with-furry-chest,
Close your mouth in smile
And curl inside to rest.

Migration

Again, you have left your solitary sleep
and journeyed on child's feet
to the warmth your sleeping mother makes,
this breathing space you've always called
your own.

Too tired to move you, I yank at the blankets
to claim back my share, to remind you
that I too, am here, grumbling to myself
'this is not the way things are supposed to be.'

And you roll toward me. Your head migrates
unerringly to that space beneath my chin
where you snuggle in as if to say
that whatever the day has been

the love that fills this bed
is more than I might claim
by right or dreams to know.

And so I fall asleep, embraced
by the breathing that fills this space
with such delicate and, yes
such undeservéd grace.

Images

In daylight, you draw unhurried lines,
give shape to forms you need to know.

When my gaze intrudes, you
stare back, as if saying "No"

We make our art differently; in early
morning hours I embrace the image of you

I draft with my pen, or stare at you
while you sleep until some inner warning

turns your back to me,
pulls your covers tight.

It is nothing so common as fright
enfolding you in its arms

but the need of a muse
yet to be known

guiding you toward
shapes, lines and images

separately your own.

Loss

It is what happens when you turn six.
Suddenly, there at the bottom of your mouth,
you place your finger on your front
left tooth and find that it wiggles.

Your eyes sparkle like sunlight
on the crest of waves as your finger,
hooked like a question mark, returns
and returns to work the top of the tooth.

I ask what you are thinking, recalling
how you always answer "nothing," or
"I wasn't thinking anything about any
one thing." But today you say,

"Well, I was thinking something,
but it's too hard to explain,"
as though growing up were ever easy,
as though, even if you understood,

you would want to explain, as though
explanations ever explained anything
as important as this.

Instead you wiggle your tooth again,
excited by the wobbling,
wriggling inside your mouth

opened as it is,
in that round "O" of awe.

Pony Tail

As she picks up
the pony tail holder,
the slant of her eyes
changes from elf to expert.
Deftly she places
a fist full of fingers
through the center
of the blue elastic,
stretches it wide
and moves her hand
to the back of her head
to meet its mirrored twin.

Three strokes of her hair
and then, with
such quickness
I'm never sure I saw it,
she pops the length of her hair
through the elastic, pushes it
back, reaches down,
grabs two fistfuls of hair,
pulls them asunder,
strokes her hair again and then

moves on to whatever is next—

as though such magic
were just an every day thing
in her six year old life,
as though you'd have to be five
not to know how to do *that!*

Shoes

Antsying about for something to do,
you come upon my shoes, lying
where I left them on the floor.

You put your feet in them,
stand and grin, then waddle
over to the sofa where I read.

It is an ancient ritual, isn't it,
this measuring of ourselves,
this stepping into our parents' shoes?

You plop yourself onto the cushion
next to me, heft those shoes up
and lay them in my lap.

I look at you,
you clown, you treasure,
you with the impish grin

who might never imagine
how much I would like
to see myself as I see you

doing the best I can
in the shoes I have put on,
lumbering around left foot, then right,

so clever, so filled with delight.

A Note to My Wife

It is an "off day" as our daughter
would say — no school. I am home
with the children. This morning
we got up late, ate peanut butter
in bed, and read.

The sun is shining after days of rain,
leaves cascade from trees
and cover the ground with a collage
of yellow, maroon and red.

Our daughter and her friend
are talking about school, about math
and times tables and how they aren't
supposed to know yet that if you
multiply backwards you are dividing.
"I learned that early," her friend says.

As I wash the dishes, I think
there is little I can recall
that I learned early,
most things I learned quite late:
how to ask for help,
to say yes, or no, and mean it,
how to be a father,
and how to love.

Today, my spirits are buoyed
by what I know and do.
I am washing dishes
and feeling grateful
for this morning, this family, and you.

Urgent, Confidential, F.Y.I.

If not for her, he tells me over lunch,
I'd probably be in administration by now,
as busy, I imagine, as the whirring
of his secretary's computer, making
important things happen like new committees,
new structures for new systems, power-point
presentations and memoranda to him
labeled *Urgent, Confidential, F.Y.I.*

But who then, would hold my hand,
walk soft-small arm in mine through
Autumn's wood noticing pine needles
tipped with gold, leaves falling red, falling
yellow, nut-gathering squirrels chattering
in oak branches, touch-me-nots springing seeds?

Who would lay a skin-soft cheek on my shoulder,
mornings so sweet as we read storybooks and poems,
laughing at pictures, at words, sending each other
syllables of love, messages like *caterpillar-tickle,*
butterfly-kiss, royal noogie, bear hug, and
crocodile tears crying

what more important than this,
what, more important, than this?

Toenails

My daughter sits beside me as I write
in my journal. She has just gotten up,

dressed and brushed her teeth. She wants
to play a game, she says, because

she is bored. But she knows I am writing
and so adds, "after you do that."

She stretches out on the sofa, watching me,
her foot jamming into my thigh.

Her toenails are sharp and need cutting
but if I ask her she will say "no."

I ask her anyway. She grimaces,
shakes her head and says:

"Do you know you have
the darkest skin in the family?"

and she grins as if to say
that we both know it is she

who will determine
how we spend this day.

Blessing

Blessed be our children
who take us out of ourselves
who teach us
even as they grow from us.

II

The Curator of Dreams

Fathers

Late at night we stand over you,
curious fathers

watching the dreams you dream
unfurl across your brows.

Your breath heaves in the cradle
of your covers

the dreams you dream
crown you other.

We walk in the waking of the night,
in our own breathing, in our own cover.

Angles of Sunlight

As I read Zen in the morning
my young daughter leaves her bed
and lies next to me on the sofa
where sunlight angles through the window.

In half-sleep, her brown eyes
stare off at the large oak
unleaving in front of the house.

I cup her head in the palm of my hand,
feel the chambers of my heart fill and empty,
fill and empty like the words on the page fill

my spirit, like the breath of her lungs
as her chest rises and falls like the leaves
on that tree, dancing in the wind and knowing,

as they know,
something important
about attachment,
about letting go.

Beginning this Day

My daughter sits at the breakfast table,
brown sugar topping her cereal. I have
been watching as she moves her grown-up
spoon from bowl to mouth to bowl again,
her brown eyes flickering, until,

almost as if by chance, she notices
me gazing at her, my smile looking
like it must when, on a clear winter's night,
I gaze beyond Orion at stars a thousand
light years away, and feel blessed

by the miracle of generations that has brought me
to just this particular moment when she hunches
her shoulders, squints her entire face and says,
"stop looking at me. Why are you
looking at me? I don't like you doing that."

I try not to feel diminished as when I look at
the distant sky and think how the light I see
may be nothing so much as a ghostly illusion
from stars that have been dead for centuries.

My daughter is almost four. At her birthday party
there will be games, ice-cream, cake and candles
that she will blow out. "You're not going to be there,"
she informs me, "because . . . . no boys."

I grin, but she reminds me again, "Stop looking at me.
I don't like you looking at me." She puts down her spoon
and covers my eyes with her hand.

Against the dark I feel the beating of my heart.
Light enough to begin this day, I think. Light enough.

Gossamer

Baruch hashaim, yaim yaim
("blessed is the name of the Lord from day to day")

Halfway between child and girl
you stretch your now long legs
the length of the sofa,
raise one hand over your head
and announce, again, "I'm bored."

But books are becoming your friends,
and summer mornings, when time permits,
we read on the sofa, side by side
or you with your head on my lap.

I relish the back and forth of your eyes
on the page, your ponytail spread
like gossamer in sunlight.

Soon you will ask for breakfast,
but now, two thumbs holding your page
in place, you read. Sun cascades
through the window, your brown hair
sparkles with flashes of red
like mine did when I was a kid.

I think of the generations of our lives—
wish you increased joy,
more grace,
less pain,
more ease.

As we read, I catch your eyes
looking at mine. They glimmer

in a way that makes me remember
the "baruch hashaim, yaim yaim"
my grandfather would say
reminding me, once again
of the blessings of this,
of every day.

Delta 1530:
He Returns to His Mother

In the airport I want to speak,
but the gate agent calls and we hug
goodbye. I watch him disappear down
the long ramp. He does not look back.

The years teach how to ignore the sadness.
When he goes there is little left to do
but follow my feet toward short term parking.

I check my watch, the shopping list in my pocket,
drive out of the lot to the nearby Safeway
where I open the door to the roar of jet engines,

look up and see his plane
reaching into the sky as I hear myself,
like a cheerleader who never quite made the team,

calling into the roar above
a celebration of this unexpected
moment for love.

The Curator of Dreams

It is, perhaps, the noose
I put my own neck in

when I go to my children thinking
I might save them

from their nightmare dreams,
and so speak their names

gently, again and again
saying, "I love you"

stroking their hair
with such priestly care

I imagine old demon truth
would not dare

to fill their ears
with my own nightmare fears

telling them what we both
have begun to understand:

that there is
nothing I can do

to ease their pain,
but whisper

these words, my prayers,
their names.

Magnificat!

Tonight, on holiday in Oxford, Bach's *Magnificat.*
The top windows of the Sheldonian are open and music
surrounds the building, drifting down Broad street
where we walk in the cool of evening's extended light.

Eva races down the cobbled path, leaps small tour jetés
on the gravel. We try to hush her exuberance,
but her grin is too full, the brightness
in her eyes too light, too light . . . .

Watching her, I think of my grandfather telling how
in the old country, near Kiev, his family locked
their doors and hid in the basement each Easter
when the Christians, leaving church, raced down
the cobbled streets of the Jews, hurling stones
and dung at anyone they saw, chanting
"Christ killer, Christ killer . . . ."

This evening, the inheritance of generations overwhelms:
the impossibility of even imagining all this,
years ago when grandfather, escaping from Russia,
knocked down a guard and ran for his life, for the life
of this very child, running with abandon,
to the sounds of the *Magnificat*—

Gloria Patri, Gloria Filio,
Gloria et spiritui sancto.

Lot 15, Lot 16

Suddenly, it seems, they appear —
signs proclaiming, "Lot 15," "Lot 16"
posted on the trees on the outskirts
of what has been your woods
for over 20 years.

Oh, you knew it could come,
there was neighborhood gossip
of a landowner in Kansas or California

who twice has sold to loggers
the largest of the oaks,
leaving behind a bramble of branches
that healed quickly enough. . .

but these signs, these were different:
you knew as soon as the men came
to clean out the undergrowth,
then the backhoe, and it would not be long
before the bulldozers and cement trucks,
the hammers and nails, drywallers,
painters and moving vans.

This landscape is changing, you think,
annoyed, saddened almost to crying,
hardly recalling when you dreamed
your own dreams here
about yourself, your family, lot nine.

Thursday: Garbage Day

Thursdays are trash collection days,
and, if you fail to remember that
on Wednesday night, Thursday mornings
are anxious because

you can never be sure what time
the trash collectors will arrive.
If you miss them, it's a whole week
of garbage rotting into sludge.

And so you get up earlier than you wanted,
grumble through the house
to empty waste-paper baskets,
check the refrigerator for moldy food,

tie up the bag and go outside to push
the big, brown Waste-Management barrel
to the street, like a kind of penance
for not planning ahead.

This morning I find myself wishing
that my other sins could be atoned for
with such ease when I notice the rosebush,
still blooming, even though it is late November.

I reach for a flower
with so little caution
I get pricked by a thorn,
pause, then carefully pluck

one for my wife's dresser,
one for my daughter's desk,
and return to the kitchen,
suddenly stunned

to think about
what this morning's garbage has brung.

At Duntulm Castle

It used to be just snuggling for its own sake,
but here on a bench by Duntulm Castle,
where the sea blows its chill wind,
my daughter snuggles in,
tells me she is cold and I am warm.

I squeeze her tight,
my right hand rubs up and down her arm
as if to build a fire.

In the distance, the Hebrides rise
through the sea mist as though
marking the border of the world.

My daughter puts her head on my belly
and, remembering our conversation from breakfast,
says with a generosity I treasure daily,
"if you lost weight, Daddy,
you wouldn't be as warm as you are."

How we define the borders of our lives,
I think, how blesséd are their mysteries.

I look out at the blue mountains,
feel the salt wind against my face,
and, not quite daring prayer

simply *wish*
to hold what's here

in this sweet embrace, forever.

Summer Dance Camp, first day

a letter to my daughter from my poetry workshop

Today we both rise from strange beds
into unfamiliar rooms, uncharted ways
—your dance, my song—
these wild infusions of art
we give ourselves to.

You are scared. Me too.
Your sweet years provide no masque for fears
but my cool, despite its practiced class,
is, at best, a dangerous craft.
Let it pass.
Today may we leap into the mystery —
a tour jeté, a poem . . . .
May we both land lightly.

I will place my words on this page,
you will point your toes. Each according to each
we arrange things, just so: 1st draft, 1st position, 4th, 5th —
each move an exploration, a master class

home, then away, plié, élevé,
extend, return, extend again.

The Shape of Things

The experience of a goldfish, I imagine,
is determined by the particular shape
of the goldfish bowl

but how much can we really know,
I wonder, thinking again of when I visited
Wales, to go where my son had been....

and how I thought of him as I got off the train
at Portmadoc, seeing that station, that street,
that phone which must have been the one
he called me from....

I looked off at the mountain cliffs.
They were steep and dangerous
and so covered in fog I could not see
the trails he climbed that night
aiming to witness dawn's first light.

And how could I have known,
to warn him,
as surely I would have done...

though truth be told,
he did just fine without me,
like the goldfish in my daughter's room

and what do I know, really,
of that goldfish, or this night

or my son, climbing his own dark paths,
seeking his own true light.

Children of Eden

Sometimes I try to imagine
what it was like for God
as he watched over the garden,
and Eve, to whom he had given
freedom and but one command.

Is it wrong to assume that she
wasn't so different
from my children, or me?

Or to think it was not defiance
so much as simple curiosity
she left as her legacy?

And how could God,
we might want to ask,
leave that choice,
that consequence,
to such innocence?

And dare we,
cradling our own sweet children,
acknowledge in them
equal freedom, equal power?
Can we, too, say, "o.k....,
well, here's the key, drive carefully,"

never knowing for sure
if they will return, or at what hour,
or what they might choose to do
with such freedom,
such illusions of power?

Report Card

When I arrive to stay the week
he meets me at the door,
his face framed by a trim beard
his left earlobe double pierced,
each hole with a thin gold ring.
He has a large chest,
a slender waist, stands straight.

He cleans, he cooks, he takes care
of the children. Each day he greets me
and when we talk he says, "I agree completely,"
or "I agree one hundred percent,"
and then he adds, "*But...*"
and shares some small qualification
that is valid, of course, and how can I
disagree with him, my brother,
after he has agreed with me?

On the third day he shows me
his eldest daughter's report card
—just arrived in the mail from college—
his daughter whom he loves with a pride
that burns from his own lost childhood;
shows me her report card saying,
"I can't let you get away without bragging
a little," handing it to me with a gray
post-it note attached.

I see the "A"s, the 3.89 GPA,
his pride/her grades, and his gray note
that reads: "What can I say?"
ready to send to his daughter.

I think of our own speechless father
to whom we never gave so much as one A,
whose words were always a small concession
to effort with a capitalized "B-U-T"
so that only what followed, mattered.

How the love of fathers gets buried
in silence, like the wet snow
falling outside my window now,
covering the earth, the trees,
their branches a lacework of clarification
without longing, without a single "but,"
as though the snow were sent simply to say,
"Notice this, how lovely the branches,
each in its articulate singleness,
each in its patterned connections,
laced like this, one to another,
to tree trunk, dark and firm."

Calling Your Name

Was there ever a "yes," my son?
Did I ever stop questioning
to gaze on you with love?
Or did I imagine
that somehow, as you slept,
you would know it was me,
standing in awe
for hours by your bed?

In my dreams, I dream you
waking. They are dreams
that whisper "yes"
to each step you take.
Hear them, I pray,
if not for your own
then for my dream's sake.

8th Grade, First Day

She was anxious
had slept fitfully during the night

I could never sleep either, I told her.
We hugged good-bye.

When she returned she was
sullen and snappy

like she had been
at the end of last year.

All summer she had healed
but today she had lost it.

Notes from her teachers
brought the reasons why:

Assignments/Grading Policy

Every assignment will have an assigned
point value. The total number of points
earned, divided by the total number of points
possible, will be calculated to determine
your grade. Follow Directions.

Class Rules/Specific Procedures

Be on Time. Take your seat and complete
the warm-up exercise. Lateness will
result in a detention slip and potential
loss of points. Follow Directions.
I dismiss the class, not the bell.
Let's have an excellent, Educational Year!

"Yea, right, sure" as my daughter might say.

I look at her sullen face. The doubt
and hurt that glaze her numb.

Her gym teacher, she reports, says "ain't"
every other sentence as in "this ain't no play time."

He makes fun of the girls,
and enjoys himself immensely.

Her math teacher spent the whole first class
telling his students how hard his course is.

"I don't want to take flute lessons this year"
she says. "I don't have time."

She is trying to sort things out.
She is scared.

The curriculum says they are teaching her
life skills, citizenship.

At dinner she complains
about the spaghetti.

***

Late that night, I pack her lunch,
write "I love you"
on a note I put with her sandwich.
Then, in parenthesis, "Bark back!"

though I know that is
not her way.

In the morning, after she leaves
I wonder what a father can do.

In the morning, after she leaves,
I write this and weep.

Going Fishing

Jacob shows me a blueberry he has just picked.
It is tinged with red, but mostly metallic blue.

He wants me to take him fishing
but I have told him he must wait
until after I finish reading my book.

I have just two more pages, but he has
been patient long enough. "Here," he says,
extending the blueberry toward me.
His eyes are bright with expectation.

"It's not quite ripe," I say.
He withdraws his offering,
pops the blueberry into his mouth
and eats it.

"Is it bitter?" I ask.
"Sour," he says.

He is silent for a long time,
then announces:
"I'm going fishing.
I'm going to get my fishing rod
and go fishing by myself."

As I continue to read
the ghost of the berry
bites bitter recriminations
against my tongue —

though it blooms in Jacob's mouth,
nurturing what he has already become.

The Apple of Your Mother's Eye

I

In a moment of idleness, I catch myself
thinking of Eden, the unnamed fruit
and that moment

when Eve first began to guess
that life might offer something more
than "yes."

Her curiosity haunts us yet.

II

On holiday, my wife and I sit in the garden
while our daughters, cartwheeling
on the lawn, call out, "Hey Mom!
Watch me, watch me, Mom!"

Why do they call to her and not to me, I wonder;

then, thinking of Eve, imagine what she
must have thought about fathers, how she
never knew the fruit of
a mother's
redeeming love.

A Father's Tale

"In the 1840's, Hans Christian Andersen fell deeply in love with the Swedish singer, Jenny Lind — also called the Swedish Nightingale. However, Jenny Lind did not return his affectionate feelings, and this unhappy love affair greatly influenced Hans Christian Andersen's work"

— an exhibit sign in Hans Christian Andersen's house,
Odense, Denmark

Nor was she the first, or last—
fairy tales are made of such longings—
we try to sort them out, write stories

of nightingales, fill the dark by pressing
flowers, cutting paper, or doodling with pens
for hours and hours. We all have fairy tales

to keep distant the demons that would dull
our hearts. We live them over and over
to keep back the dark, keep us from wondering

who we are, anyway, to protect, say,
our children, late at night: soldiers, warriors,
knights of unerring light offering safe journey

across cold and creaking floors, through shadowy
hallways to the bathroom door. Hand in hand,
our children have no fear of darker beings

or darker years, and even we, still half asleep
forget to fear what there is to fear, and so,
standing there, become a fairytale all its own,

father and child living it in the night until
the bathroom light flickers and with fatherly
pride we turn aside until the toilet's flushed

and we walk them back to bed, kisses again,
"good night, sleep tight. . ." never thinking
to blush, or recall our own uncertain fright.

III

In its Thinness, the Air is Full

This Morning

This morning, at 7:15 A.M.
I watched my youngest child
get into our car, back it into the street
and drive two tons of danger
toward her school.

The sun had barely risen.

She sat, both hands on the steering wheel,
peering through her glasses
and, as she does, driving nine miles
an hour over the speed limit so that
no one behind her will get annoyed
that she is going too slow.

It was not my eyes
so much as my prayers
that followed her out of sight,

not so much my prayers as my fright.

Vacation

Come bed time
and my wife is reading her book
and my eldest daughter is doing
leg-lifts while talking
to her younger sister
and she calls out from the other room
"Mommy, wake me early, please
so I can go to the beach
before we check out at noon."

And then I turn my bed light off
and lie on top of the cool sheets,
and I call out to my daughters,
"I love you guys"   and I turn
and stroke my wife's cheek
and say I love you to her
and she pauses from her reading
to look me right in the eye
and say, "I love you, too"

just about exactly the way
I always imagined my wife
and the mother of my children
would do.

Versions

There are few real lies, he thought.
Mostly there are versions of the truth.

He is mowing the lawn again,
back and forth, not quite retracing his steps.
With each pass, the mower blade
mangles and chops the small branches
he should have cleared from the ground.

Thinking about this
he is also thinking about the divorce
and how, after all these years,
his sons still hurt
from the uncertain constructions of things
they have been given, or imagined
and chosen to believe.

What difference does truth make,
he wonders, when what we feel is hurt

and he thinks about the grass
being clipped under the mower.
He aims only to make things tidy,
beautiful, even, though the dull blade
of his labor tears at each individual top

leaves it to heal
as best it can.

My Daughter, Dancing

(with gratitude to Sheryl-Marie Dunaway)

Suddenly, she's become a woman:
shoulder blades and arms, fingers & legs

& feet that leap, with pointed toe
She holds herself, just so.

Line, balance, bend, flow
where did my little daughter go?

Up, attitude, plié

"Pay attention to your angles.
Tendu to the back.
Let the ballet connect the steps.
Beautiful, Eva, excellent"

your teacher calls —

it is the same in second as in first
except of course, it is not,

tendu, plié, tendu, plié
tendu to first:

the toe, the knee, the hip,
rib-cage and chest

front-up, open, back up, open
tendu, plié

she moves with grace
she moves with balance and control

I watch in awe,
see more than I want to know —

tendu, plié, tendu, plié,

my dancing daughter is
dancing away.

Poem for Brian

February 10, the day the golden crocuses
rose from the ground, the day you turned 30.

I

Driving to Linda's Café

Driving to breakfast, I approach
an old Chevy Citation traveling
in the left hand lane at exactly the speed limit.

Traffic jams up around it.
Inside, a determined lady,
her face furled with scorn, drives silently

I pray that you will never be
like that, my son: so doggedly right
that anger travels like a friend, beside you.

II

Breakfast with Friends

An almost weekly ritual: Coffee,
eggs over easy, sausage (link), toast,
grits, good conversation and laughter.

How easily we slide into this booth,
talk, listen. Kindness seasons the eggs,
the chatter, the teasing banter.

III

Hiring a New Teacher

Attending a teaching demonstration
eight hours after breakfast,
we are asked to write about something
we "noticed this morning in the blur that passed."

And of course I came back to the golden crocus,
the promise of Spring, and my prayers,
offered up to the warming sun,
the old lady I smiled at as I passed,
the breakfast I ate with friends:

May your days be bright with good fortune,
my son,
may the blooming that has begun,
be without end

My Daughter Turns 18

"I'm going to sleep on Dominick's boat tonight,"
she announces. . . .
And what is my role now? What do I say?
What silences are best observed?

My mind reels: "what if this, and what if that?"
What if this guy ruins her life? Well, not ruins it,
I think, but. . . . she has such potential!
Possibilities stretch before her—

I can't control the father in me, blurting out,
blurting on and on. . . . And this fellow, this
Dominick! A sweet boy, no doubt, but
must he spend every moment of the day
and night with my daughter, must he love her
so unconditionally she turns blind as stone?

"You're a flower," I want to say,
"a sprig just potted in rich soil.
You're blind with infatuation.
Get a Grip!" I want to yell.

But I calm myself. Such words would hurt,
her eyes would well up, her unsullied spirit
flinching back,

"What do you know?!" she would snap,
"what do *you* know about love?"
Insistent, demanding — a question my age
has begun to suggest I ask myself

as daily I confront my failures, as here too,
with her: What *do* I know about love?

I fall silent, dumb.
I turn to prayer.
It is my last, best hope,
perhaps my only hope.

"Dear Lord," I mumble to myself,
"Dear Lord!"

Icarus

After a month of traveling,
our daughters have gone off by themselves
to make the rocky and narrow trek
from Vernazza to Monterosso del Mare,
the most difficult climb in the Cinque Terre,
the one that enables them, gracefully,
to leave their doting parents behind.

"Yes," I tell my wife
when she asks, "I think they'll be fine.
And anyway, what choice do we have?"

We sit on a terrace overlooking the Mediterranean
sipping cappuccino while our daughters are off,
climbing rocks without us.

Clouds move in, then a chill wind. My wife says,
"I hope they make it to the next town before it rains."
Which they will and then return,

just five minutes by train, with stories to tell –
wide-eyed with confidence and pride,
excited to do it again.

Later, turning in for the night,
my wife and I will hold each other tight
while upstairs our children dream
of their next adventure,
their next flight.

I Wake Early

I wake early to sunshine sliding
through the shuttered window.

My family is still asleep
cooing like pigeons – or are those pigeons,
calling to each other outside the window?

Traveling, things begin to blur.
We are squeezing too much
into too many places.

Take this morning, for example:
It is cloudy, the air is chilly, the laundry
needs to be done but Venice lies before us.

Dare we wash our clothes? Cut our toenails?
Have a bowl of plain spaghetti,
attend that Vivaldi concert this evening,
and go to sleep early?

The sun brightens.
My wife returns from her bath.
My youngest stretches herself into the world.
Church bells ring outside the window
as she yawns "morning, daddy."

Whose heart would not gladden
at such communion?

Along the canals and across the bridges,
everything is as permanent as motion,
like us, traveling in this quadrangle of lives.
The wind cascades along the cobblestones,
singing.

Departures

When I used to linger at the airport
studying the plane that carried my sons away,
I liked to imagine I was standing watch
there on the observation deck,
blessing their flight with fatherly love
and sending them off with angels

but always there was that moment —
the aircraft underway, its arching turn
setting a course against which my eyes
were squinched —

when the plane suddenly disappeared
crashing into my parent-fears,
confronting my love-mythology
to remind me again how much
I must trust what I cannot see.

And how small I'd feel then, do feel,
knowing this, knowing that no matter
what I wish, there are limits,
squinty-eyed points at which even
my own children become utterly other

like these small clouds
passing wispily before me now,
how the speed of their flight does not alter
even as they evaporate,
vanish imperceptibly, from my sight.

Breathing

"Daddy, I can't sleep."
"Why not?"
"I keep thinking about that movie."
"What would you like me to do?"
"I don't know, what do daddies usually do?"

****

And so I walk her back to bed,
snuggle next to her like daddies do,
I suppose, to help her fall asleep.

The fingers on my right hand feel
the flesh of her delicate ear
where the pierced lobe speaks

of the womanhood she has been
as impatient to grow into as she
has been impatient with me

when I have not been for her
what we both imagine daddies
are supposed to be.

Side by side the body
of a young woman,
the body of an older man.

Our very breath feels dangerous.
I push myself up on my elbows, kiss
her forehead and say a soft goodnight.

She is breathing steadily as I close
the door behind me, tight.

Winter Break

(our daughter returns from college)

She swoops in from the South
expectant and expecting.
She brings seeds and berries,
fruits freshly plucked
if not necessarily ripe.

Excited by the harvest
she dances her dance —
old steps and new
brighten our nest like sunlight
rising through the winter's gloom.

She gathers with her friends.
They come and go

though
when they leave

they will return to that new place
they already call their home.

***

Life here goes on, but the house is quiet.
In the silence she leaves behind, we read.
At dinner we talk of her in reverent tones
say grace, give thanks.

Even in its thinness, the air is full.
Remembrance is weighty.
The future is weighty.
Of this we take and eat.

Wishing

It was the tears in her eyes,
how they filled with her sadness,
as she turned to me
and, knowing better, still asked,
"Daddy, why is this happening?
How can we stop it?"

And of course I had no answer.
I tried one, meekly, and she shot me
one of her looks as if to say
don't give me that daddy-crap.
This is important,
I'm asking for answers!

She knew there were none
and that I knew that too.

I held her, both of us crying our loss
both of us holding on to each other
— daddy and daughter —
wishing there were only that.

The Given World

(in the aftermath of 9/11)

On the plate of what was once the future,
the present.

It is not what I hoped it would be.
My anguish frightens me.

Tears well their apology
my gut is sick with rage.

This is not the world for which
– when you were born –
I prayed.

Promises

I

The promises I made to my firstborn,
cradling his infant body and praying
that he might somehow learn to swim
in that noisy world we'd given him. . . .

What, really, could I see of him then?
His bald head, his wrinkled skin,
The cracks of my own failures
already gathering along the edges
of my dreams?

II

Nearing 50, I learned to face my own father,
to see his frail and fragile light,
the years of trying and failing
and trying again: to see that he is human,
and loves as best he can.

And I think of my own sons,
how we have struggled
and bent and turned,
and how, slowly, we have learned
the comfort of each embrace,
the blessing of each other's human face.